POEMS 31

POEMS 31

Chapters 1–3
...beginning with the first verse.

Chapter 4 – <u>Bonus</u> Chapter and Verse
Chapter 5 – Special <u>Added</u> Feature -
"Animal Crackers"

Donald Anthony King

ARPress
ILLUMINATING IDEAS
EMPOWERING VOICES

ARPress
45 Dan Road Suite 5
Canton MA 02021
Hotline: 1(888) 821-0229
Fax: 1(508) 545-7580

Ordering Information:
Quantity sales.Special discounts are available on quantity purchases by corporations, associations, and others.For details, contact the publisher at the address above.

Printed in the United States of America.

ISBN-13:	Softcover	979-8-89330-598-2
	eBook	979-8-89330-599-9

Library of Congress Control Number: 2024902484

Tribute

*From the family
of
Alphonso L. King, Sr.
&
Velma J. King*

Trust in the Lord with all your heart, and lean not on your own understanding; in all your ways acknowledge him, and he will make your paths straight.

Proverbs 3:5-6

Prelude

Don't Even Go There!

"Father, you say that I'm invincible............

and you know, I can even walk on water.

I really don't see what the problem is -

I just wanna..........chill, get some (R & R)

rest and relaxation from my daily responsibilities."

"There, no one will bother me, unless I change water

into wine – and someone might say," "Hey! Buddy,

you got any ice, I'm burning up down here!!!"

"Do you hear anyone singing?" "I'll take you there!"

"No, you don't, so get over it!" "Who in their right mind

would actually – GO TO HELL!!"

"Like I told you before." "Don't even go there!"

(With a thundering Echo resound/reverberation):

I AM _your_ Father!!

Chapter 1

Table Of Contents:

Ubiquity of the Futuristic

I'm in flight, despite a night's forecast,
of Mother Nature's finest moment.
I too, as no other, can renounce the thought,
of my arrival, mistaken for a landing.
I keep within me, a key to time......
and shield life and away all its legends.
I have no effects on the elements of earth,
but trickling sand is to my liking; however.

Meeting in the Elbow Room

It all started—when I laid an egg,
with a race upstream, you know.
I pushed, I tugged and juxtapositioned
myself, with only......5 months to go.
The lake is big—ocean wide,
with a bellowing of sounds, you know.
I found myself—flipped upside down!
with only......10 weeks to go.
I don't know why, I slip and slide,
my grip isn't so good, you know.
Do you mind? if I flush the line,
and feel the warm water flow.
Now, it's time—this wet-n-wild ride,
is splitting the wishbone broom.
At last!! I gasped, to stretch out my hands
and get more elbow room.

Poor man's diet

1 slice of wheat bread—cut thrice.
The bacon drippings don't drip,
don't taste so nice.
The last egg in the house, beaten twice.
With all we have left—one cup of rice.
Only tap water to drink—
add two (2) cubes of ice.
Can't buy whole milk, not at that price.
Meat not an option, substitute
a cheese slice.
No potatoes to cook, only one (1) carrot
to dice.
Look at Hungry!
sitting at the kitchen table,
waiting all-day for a *syrup sandwich* to entice.
But on the poor man's diet—
your calorie intake, is the……
tightening grip of a stomach vice.

Rich man's diet

Two (2) bottles of champagne—poured twice.
Jumbo shrimp wrapped in bacon,
so tight, so nice.
Crab meat-lumped crepes, folded thrice.
Oysters on the half-shell, chilled on ice.
Crawfish Etouffee, served over rice.
Saffron and lemongrass, added for spice.
Steak and lobster ordered—at market price.
Only, a vintage pinot noir will suffice.
Look at Jelly-roll!
Lounging in the dining room,
all-dressed up in black-tie.
As for the rich man's diet—
your appetite—is the <u>best</u>—money can buy.

Dx: Crippled (Part I)

Though you call me cripple—
I <u>never</u> see you laugh.
You label me handicapped—
despite your malcontent.
I've been told—I need assistance,
as you extend your credit line.
Though, I'm classified disabled,
while you—drink, smoke, get high.
So you say, I'm a cripple
.........medically speaking, so—
But whose life is really crippled?
I guess…you don't know.

Footnote: Dx—medical abbreviation for diagnosis.

Crippled and Handy-capped (Part II)

You say, I am crippled
……yet you refute, you are not.
You say—I am helpless.
You don't know, your own crutch.
You say—I am hopeless,
but your drinking, seems non-stop.
Before you say, I am crippled,
with a handicapped slobber and a swig.
Yes, I am crippled!
#!!?@#!*You intoxicated disgusting pig!!

Bottle Stopper Mash

Wobble and a dance—
to a bottle cap twist.
Sucking beer foam
in a mystifying mist.
Jumping to the top shelf—
sitting in the mix.
Throwing back a shot,
with a sugar-rim fix.
Slipping off the barstool,
near the swinging door.
Sipping on a Mai Tai—
on the lighted floor.
Pumping your fist
and slapping down cash.
Popping your cork,
to the Bottle Stopper Mash.

Some days

Some days......I feel like killing myself.
Some days......I feel like praying out loud.
Some days......I feel like watching cartoons.
Some days......I feel like watching the news.
Some days......I feel like mowing the lawn.
Some days......I feel like cutting the grass.
Some days......I feel like going to work.
Some days......I feel like staying at home.
Some days......I feel like calling a friend.
Some days......I feel like writing a poem.
Some days......I feel like.........
                    Some days.

Non-profit Organization

Dear charter member,
This is a non-profit organization—
Please send proceeds to:
the Chief Executive Officer,
the Chief Operating Officer,
the Chief Financial Officer,
not to mention the President,
Vice-President and
Janitor (who is also
the Treasurer and Secretary).
Remember, this is a
non-profit organization!
If in doubt, send proceeds to:
Lock Box #777.

Deceitfully yours,
Chairman and Founder

Wipe your tears

Doesn't want to remember......
Every time her name is mentioned.
After many years together—
They separated unexpectedly;
He has been crying ever since.

Imagine...his pain, shocking disbelief!
Since his Sierra truck was towed away.

Window pain

Your reflection in the mirror, reveals
a crack, but the mirror is not cracked,
you see.
The smokescreen which clouds your way
of life, is a delusionary mask to me.
Looking high up in the sky, you notice
a cloud or two.
Puffy clouds are all around, while
nightfall inhales your coo.
The rock through the window, conceals a crack,
but the window pane is not broken, you see.
Your psychedelic habit of destroying
yourself, is a very painful sight to me.

Whether Report

I don't know *whether* I like you,
or I just like having you around.
I don't know *whether* or not I need you,
or maybe—it's because you want me.
Regardless, I never question whether I'm
better off with you—or without you.
I know for sure, I would be okay,
whether or not you needed me.
However, we've both managed—
to *weather* the storm.
And now for the *weather*.........
Today's forecast.........a cold day in Hell!!
Now stay tuned for your nightly local news,
back after a short station break.

Chapter 2

Table of Contents:

Spectacular! Spectacular!

He dreamed of fortune and fame.
All he got was frustration and pain.
Spectacular! Spectacular!
His world........is like an oyster,
but it's all clammed up inside.
A whimsical plight he finds his life;
beset with opportunities gone aside.
Spectacular!! Spectacular!!
The money he yearns, for caviar and foie gras—
compares to nothing he earns, for a
second-hand used car.
He solemnly sits, watching his favorite sports teams.
Let it be known—here dies all his hopes and dreams.
Spectacular!!! Spectacular!!!

Footnote: foie gras pronounced *fwa*—*'gra*\\ like Mardi gras.

Passion Fruit Sweet Tea

Dressed to impress—he combs
his favorite night scene.
She dons a cap and black
leather-trimmed blue jeans.
As he waits on his date,
he dances and twirls.
She stopped short of setting—
any of her hair up in curls.
Gathered at the bar,
his gender spreads.........
However, she doesn't see him
among the same-like threads.
Though, both may order
a drink or two—or three.
But his and her drinks
together—cannot be.
Since…he likes he—
and she likes she.
Last call is with the bartender,
each of them sees;
"May I have a Passion Fruit Sweet Tea,
would you please!"

Sunday Best

He sits alone in the chair, like a mannequin—
listening to the people, quietly walk in.
His sweaty palms are tucked in beside him,
as his prayer to the Almighty Father begins.
Dear God, can you ever forgive me,
for I knew I should not have sinned.
Please make room for me in heaven ~
I promise, the killing spree will soon end.
He sat upright as people watched him,
try to position his jacket straight.
The man next to him raised his hand!
. . . . to electrocute the inmate.

Lipstick; burning

A lit smoke in the mouth,
parts a tongue-n-cheek kiss.

Puckered in to draw—
putting your lungs both at-risk.

Breathing in relaxes, but
stops!—a dead man his.

Nicotine calls your name,
luring its fan club—*amiss.*

Soothing sweet tobacco—
for your pleasure zone bliss.

Life can be a drag;
if smoking is all this (is).

Ho-tell chain

This franchise stays open for business;
busy at bedtime—during the week.
Never closes early on Sunday,
since time-sharing is…at its peak.
Nighttime employs the company—
working hours; accordingly so.
Time manages the flow of output,
as jobs come and steadily go.
These ladies never balk—about overtime.
Never mind, time-and-a-half.
Don't bother writing down double-time.
Pay-scales are based on their craft.
Pounding the pavement in high heels.
Dress code: business street-wise.
Always in search of a money-making deal.
A sales call at the nearest high rise.

Financially!.........challenged

Swimming in debt—
Not wanting to get my hair wet.
Financially strapped—
Not having to wear a money belt.
Money unkind—
Not able to really give a dime.
Signature loan—
Reason denied—account on hold.
Bills past due—
Not a trying attempt......to collect a few.
Pawn shop, I think—
Easy blood money—forged in red ink.
Credit card instead—
Short-cut to financial debt ahead.
Time it seems—
What I need, to put my mind at ease.
Cash I need—
For the love of money, not greed.
Financially sound—
Now, I'm banking on my future-bound!!

I Heal Good!

I heal good—
'cause my health insurance
plan is so good now!
I heal good—
'cause I'm covered like
I know that I should now!
So good! it should!!
(since) I chose you!
I heal nice!
I had a sex change twice.
I heal—nice!!
with my doctor's advice (now)!
So nice! it feels nice!!
(since) I have you!!
When I fold out—my—arms,
your needle will do me no harm,
......and when I fold out my arms,
my coverage will do me no wrong!!
('cause) I heal good!
my doctor said I would (now)!
I heal nice!
with anesthesia and ice.
It's real—nice!!
at a Co-pay price!
Otitis!! Arthritis!!
I got you!!!

Weeping Pillow

Sad as it seems, your pillow talks,
in tongues only spoken while sleep.
You toss and turn to argue your point,
but all you do is weep.
Could it be……......a crying game?
played by one-on-one.
Or is it simply—a bad night's sleep,
awoke by the rising sun.
As I sit and listen,
in the midst of a sleepless night.
All I need to know is—
will you be alright.
Have you always felt
such heart-wrenching thoughts—
too troubling to let go?
I'm deeply hurt and sad to know—
you no longer find comfort in me.
Only solace upon a weeping pillow.

Couch Potato Recipe

Comfortably sit one (1) 300-lb man (or smaller)
on the couch—fully clothed (of course!)
Wrap snugly in a blanket (......and no
pig-in-the-blanket jokes please!)
Open two (2) bags of potato chips (low-carb <u>my</u>
<u>as</u>surance of a more balanced diet.)
Place within arms' reach—a 2-liter
bottle of diet soda (why bother?)
Okay, replace with a 3-liter bottle of
regular soda and a six-pack of beer
(........now we're talking!)
Add pretzels and salted peanuts to taste.
He should consciously monitor his
calorie intake (yeah right!)
He must be able to physically lift
the remote control and purposely aim
directly at the TV screen. Click on
Power and proceed to mindlessly
watch TV for hours. Couch potato
is done when stuffed in bed.

The Fat Lady Sing-Along Remix

"Feeling good about myself.
Candy stores—I raid the shelf.
Ate a pizza,
drank a milkshake
……..and it shows!"
Background singers—
take it to the bridge.
"Looking good and you know it!"
(...And the audience applauded!)
"She good!!"

Dinner by Candlelight

Set in the distant countryside,
not too far from theather hill.
Your table for one awaits—
in the excavated dirt fill.
When nearing the war-torn city's skyline—
please stay clear of the torch-lighted flask.
Be prepared leaving your bunker,
to don a ready-to-wear gas mask.
While waiting your turn—
to square dance with the enemy—
as planned in positioned groups.
Conflict continues to paint-ball
the town blood-shot red,
even wounding our brave troops.
Wartime keeps a ticking—
only your rifle scope keeps time.
The bullet-fire heard at nightfall,
always postpones dinnertime.
When gunfire stops for a waning moment,
though still loyal to the freedom fight.
You heat up a MRE (Meal, Ready-To-Eat)
to have dinner by candlelight.

Lloyd's Prayer

My father......you know I'm only seven.
Howard be my last name.
My Mama has come home—
I don't know what I've done.
She went to buy a loaf of bread.
Now that she's back from 7-Eleven.
Please forgive me for trying to pass
the football......and forgive those
who tried to pass the football to me.
Lead us into my room for PlayStation—
but call us when the pizza is delivered
(it's under my Mama name, Gloria).
'Cause my Mama house is clean and
she needs time to shower...........
but not forever and ever.
Amen.

Chapter 3

Table of Contents:

Can I get an Amen! (Part I)

Pass the collection plate down the line.
It's filling up quite nicely—one more time.
Deacon Paul—is it time to pray for our sins?
No! Brother! let's wait until the last row puts in.
Deacon Paul, Mrs. Sugarfoot's son, *Ben-Her*,
did it to us again!
Yes, Brother, I watched *he-she*
make change of a ten—once again.
Pastor Tooloud—go ahead! and preach us a sermon.
Well,......I went to the store. Yeah!
      I bought a ham. Yeah!
      I cooked the ham. Yeah!
      I smoked the ham. Yeah!
      I ate the ham. Yeah!
      Can I get an Amen!

Lady in Red

Found lying face down in a glass—
clinging to a stalk in the room.
Dabbed lightly in Tabasco sauce,
like an expensive cheap perfume.
She knows just how to please you;
especially when morning dew.
She wakes you up to hang over—
with vodka and tomato juice.
So—soothing and caressing—
she soaks a quenching thirst.
She stirs herself quite nicely,
with her ribbed feet extended first.
This lady has a slight condition;
so bloody to the virgin mix.
Let's just call her Bloody Mary—
garnished simply with a lemon twist.

The N-word

In most circles, this word is unspoken—
never to be confused with consent.
Definitely defined as a negative term.
On a white sheet, thumbs down is a hint.
Such a powerful word, whenever it's used,
whether directed at someone you know.
Since generations past—
left their mark, don't get hung-up
on a quest for denial.
Just take time to reveal the source of
discern, even though it might take awhile.
The N-word we speak of—has been
linked many times, as a response or
as a no-show.
But when we circle the letter
of this two-letter word—
it always stands for No!

White Trash

Be it paper, plastic, cups or knives—
forks, spoons and paper plates.
One-time usage is its mere convenience,
unlike *exquisite* <u>white</u> *bone china plates.*
Such disposable utensils do come in all colors.
Separate to recycle—or collect some for cash.
Since it seems—*<u>white</u>* is the color mostly purchased.
Can these throw-away items be considered white trash?

Mispelled

I tryed two baek u a kake,
butt I kneeded to egggs.
I wantted too frie u sum chikin;
hour ever I donut half ani flower.
I thoutt u wood lyke a baeked potatoe,
sew I wint too thee grosseri stor.
Wood u lyke four mee two
bye u a staek?
No, I would like for you to buy
a dictionary and a thesaurus.
And a thesaurus...............
(just in case you're wondering!)
...........is not a dinosaur.
Welle, bee dat whey thenn!!

Footnote: Misspelled is the correct spelling.

Money, you don't know me

I summon you into my possession,
but you bluff my hand with your poker face.
Always sought after in such high demand,
...........regardless of the currency rate.
You manage to find dual comfort—
in a wallet and even a purse.
Ever realized......when you run out—
is when it really hurts!
When I try to introduce myself,
you just turn your pompous head.
You act like you would much rather...
be with someone else instead.
That's why you and I—
don't have a good working relationship.
Have you ever spent the time of day
with me—or even bothered to leave a tip?
Now, I know what I should have known,
and it makes me want to cry.
Money, you don't know me...
and you're determined not to try.

Can I get an Amen! (Part II)

What a lovely congregation!
Look at Mrs.Sugarfoot's twin sons,
Ben-Her and *Ben-Gay* -
pretty in pink again!!
Deacon Paul is it time to deliver the message?
Pastor Tooloud – go ahead! and preach us a sermon.
Well..............I went to the hospital - Yeah!
To visit the sick and shut-in -Yeah!
As I went inside the room - Yeah!
I knelt down unnoticed at first - Yeah!
I placed my hand and blessing on her - Yeah!
And then I prayed for her - Yeah!
All of sudden! I had a revelation!! Yeah!
An angel-like voice appeared before me, and said,
"Pastor, do you know that I am the Head Nurse,
and you're in the Nurses Station."
Can I get an Amen!

Chapter 4
Bonus Chapter and Verse

Table of Contents:

Off-The-Wall Section

Knock! Knock!

<u>Knock! Knock!</u>
Who's there?
It's me, the door.

Knock! Knock!
Who's there?
It's me, the door.

Knock! Knock!
Look! If this is some kind of <u>sick</u> knock! knock! joke,
or silly game you two are playing, then someone is
(literally) banging the crap out of me.

I dare you to <u>knock! knock!</u> one more time! (silence)
Just walk away, while you still can!

Remember Me!

Unnoticeable I see, is my call to claim.
    Time need not stop, for fifteen minutes of fame.
Though the pursuit has been measured -
    over a period of time.
The recognition has been elusive,
    never suitable in-kind.
Now I stand tall, to face the disappointments ahead.
    Trusting my LORD, listens to each prayer said.
The love he has shown, cannot be denied.
    With my blessings, I do feel quite satisfied.
But to experience that incredible moment set free.
    Please GOD, just a reminder........remember me!

(Homeless) Fashion Show EXTRAVAGANZA!

Coming down the runway is Luther!

Luther is rocking a ruffled T-shirt, under his torn & tattered overalls.

Luther strike a pose! now grab your <u>one</u> shoe, as you leave the runway.

Look! at Peggy strutting down the runway.

She's wearing a two-piece jogging suit -

Faded grey in color, just a little sloppy and loose-fitting -

But the shopping cart she's pushing really sets it off!

Now, here comes Betty and Jamal, walking the runway.

Looks like Jamal is lost! (He might be looking for the food pantry).

Making a fashion statement! the spotlight is <u>on</u> Betty, as she strides down the runway.

Betty is wearing - a (fuzzy) herringbone hooded jacket,

with flannel pajama-like bottoms, and a seer-sucker top.

She completes her look, with a dis-colored scarf, gathered around the neck.

Jamal is equally as stylish and (quite) debonair in an old & weathered Navy pea-coat.

Underneath his pea-coat, he dons a (baggy) sweat suit, with an elastic waist.

As Jamal spins, the pea-coat opens up,

displaying an assortment of daily essential needs, like a traveling overnight kit.

These <u>two</u> show-stoppers know how to work the runway!

This <u>does</u> conclude the (homeless) fashion show Extravaganza!

This modeling troupe will be appearing <u>nightly</u> – underneath the bridge.

No autographs please! but donations are <u>always</u> accepted!!

Grab a seat & enjoy the show!

FWD

Fear, Worry & Doubt -
you're no longer
my best friends.

Now go on - git!

Kill-joy, no more!
.......go and harass someone else.

Behold!
I'm a child of The Most High GOD,
whose power is limitless!!
So I ain't got time to fool around with the
likes of you.

You'll need to pack your bags -
and catch the first bus out-of-town.

Now go on - git!

When you believe in yourself - there is no <u>fear</u>!
When you trust GOD - you need not <u>worry</u>!
When you have faith - there is no <u>doubt</u>!

Words of Wisdom

Trial and Error

How do you plead?
You were caught red-handed,
and arrested for breaking and entering.
"Your Honor, I was framed. They forgot to leave a key."

Defense, call your first witness.
Defense calls.................Judge Thatcher (to the stand).
"I can't testify – I'm presiding!"
Since you have no witnesses.

Defense ....how do you plead?
Oh! no! he didn't!!
Has the jury reached a verdict?
Oh! yes! he did!!

Do you want fries with that?

Can I take your order?
You know that I'm a Sommelier,
though I've been <u>called</u> a cheap wine connoisseur;
they <u>claim</u> I lack the necessary credentials to be certified.
Can you say? I'm drunk! in three different languages.

Can I interest you in a bottle of wine from our <u>exclusive</u>
local supplier, in-store, next door at 7-Eleven. I highly
recommend the <u>special</u> roast duck, with the foie gras pâté -
along with an inexpensive bottle of cheap wine. You are
(more than) welcome to BYOB, while you wait on your order.

Since I'm only <u>qualified</u> to be your waiter -
I'm not <u>allowed</u> to speak to you in three different languages.
How do you say? with a certain *je ne sais quoi* -
Do you want fries with that?

Chef Mabel "Susie" P. Craig
(a.k.a. Sweet Pea)

I don't know what's wrong with my sister-Jenny
……………………..but 'round here, we eat!
You won't find neck-bones and pig-feet on her menu.
Honey, my sister will plop! a dollop of cottage cheese
on top of a puffed rice cake, and call it dinner.
Then she wants you to pay for it!
I can hear her now! Isn't it nutritious and delicious?
…….and you're like (Yuk!) I sho' could go for some
neck-bones and pig-feet right about now!
(with a side order of fatback!)
As for me, I refuse to talk to my sister about what she does for a living.
I ain't got time to hear her carry on about me losing weight.
Look! I'm big-boned, plus-size and happy!
(with one finger snap and a circle).
Jenny Craig ain't got nothin' on me!

Twisted Sister

A woman of mystery
Difficult to predict
The category of strengths
Until she hits!!
Packing a destructive wallop!
With her wicked sister-like ease
No favoritism is <u>ever</u> shown
Along the path of people she greets
She arrives in an uproar
Quite jumpy and upset
But she leaves combing her wet hair softly
Without any (lasting) regret -

Hurricane warning: Don't get it Twisted, Sister!

Butter Melts

Charred and disfigured
Flame-<u>kissed</u> to a crisp
Unable to feel the scorching burn
Through the rising smoky mist
Sizzled by an unsightly baste
Underneath the fleshy touch
The lingering fire slowly embers
As butter melts...............as butter melts

Blistering heat crackles the skin
And all hair-raising exposed, susceptible to singe
But the meaty layers of fat, are gently peeled back
To inject with a marinade syringe
The lingering fire glowingly embers
As butter melts...............as butter melts

Snugly covered in a moist blanket
Of leaves and earthy ground
Releasing hot smoldering smoke
With coal-like rocks abound
The Kalua Pig is almost ready
Cooked perfectly to a burnt-brown
The lingering fire continues to ember
As butter melts.............as butter melts

"Cooking with Jerry"

Today, we are having a "_Cooking_" demonstration,
on how to prepare <u>hot dog water</u>!
Please take notes – if you like.
First, we place a small pot on the stove.
Can you back up!? I think I missed the first step.
Let me start over! (for those of you who didn't get it!)
I am <u>placing</u> a small pot filled half-way with tap water, on the stove
Hold up! (please). Do we season the water with sugar & spices?
No, it's just <u>plain</u> tap water.
Next, put three to four hot dogs in the pot of boiling water.
I'm confused!!? Can you put the hot dogs in the pot,
before you add the <u>water</u>? It doesn't matter!!
Now, simmer on medium heat for about -
7 to 10 minutes………..And there you have it! <u>Hot dog water</u>!!
Are there any questions?
I thought we were <u>tasting</u> fried baloney sandwiches!?
DID YOU! see me <u>preparing</u> fried baloney sandwiches!!?
Are you hungry? Come on up here!
Let me <u>bake</u> you a <u>classic</u> beef wellington,
with steamed broccoli on the side.
Would you like that!!?
Oops!! I'm sorry! - the (cooking) demonstration, is <u>now</u> over!
How 'bout a hot dog!?

Why?

Shrouded in controversy.
Smothered in negativity.
Blanketed under a cloud of gloom and doom.
Tossed into a sea of lost hope.
Depressed from a discouraging spirit.
Longing with heart-felt emotion -
he gazes (intently) into the looking glass of broken dreams,
casting a shadow and ghostly image -
of pity and self-doubt.
He then looks up, sympathetically up above
and asks, in such a painful,
yet painstakingly-like sigh!
Why?

<u>Blood</u> Thirsty!

Just looking over your application -
    for the <u>Blood</u> <u>Bank</u> <u>Director</u> (position).
Can I call you by your first name? "<u>Count</u>."
Have you <u>ever</u> worked in the Medical field?
    I <u>have</u> drawn blood before!
If you don't mind me asking? Are <u>you</u> okay?
Your <u>face</u> is turning <u>a whiter shade of pale</u>!
    I'm just a <u>little</u> thirsty!
Would you like a bottle of water?
No, thanks! I'm on a <u>special</u> liquid diet.
I see! you can <u>only</u> work the night shift.
    This might not be a good fit (for us).
We conduct our <u>blood drives</u> during the day.
Are you "squeamish" at the sight of blood?
    That is the least of your worries!
I guess, we can go ahead! and set-up a 2nd interview.
I'm not sure how to pronounce your last name.
    Just call me Drac! (for short).

Parting Shot

Testimonial:

<u>Wine-taster</u>
Am I a Sommelier -
or something like that?
From Pinot Noir to Pinot Grigio -
Cabernet Sauvignon to White Merlot.

Disclaimer:

You ain't no wine-taster.
You don't even get paid!
You're a ? # ! ? # ! goddam drunk!

<u>PCBA Binding Contract</u>
(**P**imps **C**ollective **B**argaining **A**greement)
As set forth in the by-laws,
of our collective bargaining agreement.
! ! : # ? * ! You better have my money!
Woman, (expletive! can be substituted)
You better have my money!!

Soliloquy of a Drunk Man

I'm drunk!
Yes, I'm drunk!
Let me see............if I'mmmm
    <u>really drunk</u>?!!
    I drank
A 6-pack of beer – Yep!
A bottle of wine – Yep!
Two bottles of wine – Yep!
1 liter of booze – Yep!
A bottle of water? _Wait a minute?!!_
<u>_I need a moment!_</u> (to think?!) -
Oh Yeah! I'm drunk!
I'm <u>REALLY</u> drunk!!

Chapter 5
Special <u>Added</u> Feature - "Animal Crackers"

<u>Table of Contents:</u>

- Poetic Ending -

Andre', the "Drag Queen" Gorilla

Andre' dah-ling! – How do you do it?
You look so fabulous, up on stage.

Well, Ms. Thang – let me show you how I do the damn thang!
Sashay! Swar ray!

Don't tell anyone, but I'll share (with you)
some of my beauty secrets.
The complete line of Gorilla Tape and Gorilla Glue products.

Who does your hair and make-up?
The Paint and Body Shop (down the street)
does my hair and make-up.

You look like you spent a fortune on yourself!
It's hard to look this good, without my Gorilla Tape.
I swear by it! This tape pulls it all together!
Sashay! Swar ray!

Bartholomew, the Hood Rat

Oh! I'm so refined!

Living up-scale in my double-wide.

With plush velvet paintings on the wall.

Come inside and look around!

Can I offer you some of these scrumptious hors d'oeuvres?

I'm so FANCY!! I eat (my) Vienna sausages,

with a toothpick (with my pinky (finger) extended!)

You too, can live the lifestyle(s) of the rich & famous.

Let me give you a few tips –

To keep the Joneses from looking in –

Cover your windows in tin-foil.

It adds such an exquisite touch.

For that art deco décor, remove all tires from your automobile, and

mount it-on concrete blocks (in the driveway); preferably, a Cadillac -

if you can afford such a lavish lifestyle.

Ultimately, the *pièce de résistance,* is placing

an old refrigerator on the front porch,

to create that avant-garde look!

Excuse me please! I have a phone call.

Architectural Digest? Yes, it is! Sir, we have decided

not to include your home in this month's issue.

Too much bling?!! Just, a little too much!

Don't call us – we'll call you!

Beatrice, the QUEEN Bee

She is such a <u>you know</u> what!
Making us gather nectar to make her honey.
I don't feel like making no <u>damn</u> honey!
All-day long – we fly from flower to flower,
collecting nectar for her ungrateful beehind.
She could at least help us!
I feel ya!
I have an idea to fix her lip-smackin' appetite.
Look! here's some poison oak and poison ivy blossoms.
Lets make (her) some <u>tainted</u> honey.
Wait until she taste this!!
Pucker up, Sweetheart!

Bernard, the "5-star dining" Buzzard

It's tough – being a food critic.
Unfortunately, I have to taste (and sample)
everything run-over on the highway.
Today's road-kill, is slightly <u>under</u> run-over.
It looks quite chewy, but delectable.
It could have been a bit more <u>smashed</u>,
for my liking.
All in all, each bite was quite pleasing to the palate.
For me, this roadside dining experience,
was somewhat disappointing -
because it was <u>not</u> completely run-over.
Therefore, I can only give it - 4 out of 5 stars.
Sorry!

Bubba, the Sleepless Bear

I can't sleep!! I can't sleep!! I've been
up for four months now.................and I just can't
fall asleep!! Maybe, if I count sheep.
Oh! I forgot -
I ate them all, before I went to bed.
(Does it look like I'm hibernating?!!) - I'm <u>still</u> woke!

Buster, the Brown Bear,
with the "good" hair

We're conducting Circus auditions today!
Who's next? Send him in. Your name please!
I'm Buster, the Brown Bear, with the "good" hair.
Have you ever performed for the circus? Is it like the zoo?
…...Because Buster don't do nothin'!!
Do you have any animal-trained skills (like bouncing a ball)?
Let me repeat myself, Buster <u>don't do nothin</u>' - because I'm Buster,
the Brown Bear, with the "good" hair!
Well, I'll tell you what we're looking for -
a bear who can unicycle on a high wire holding an umbrella.
Do I look like a <u>stupid</u> animal trick (to you)?!!
Before I <u>bounce</u>. Hold that thought. Let me sleep on it!
I'll get back to you in about 4 months.
Okay! Mr. Brown Bear.
The name is Buster! Buster, the Brown Bear, with the "good" hair.

Buford, the One-Tooth Alligator

Fish tease and taunt him, since he can't clamp down
to catch his food, with his one tooth. Na! NaNaNa Na!
Look! It's Buford, the One-Tooth Wonder! We'll see
who's still laughing, when I get my <u>new</u> dental implants,
specifically designed with you in mind, with fish-biting
capabilities, tested and approved – while submerged
under (murky) water. Comes with a money-back guarantee,
so I can get my crunch & munch on! I can see it now -
Fish Beware! Swim at your own risk!

Since there is no threat-level, until all your dental work
is done - I guess, you would like to entertain the thought
of inviting us all <u>over</u> for dinner. Absolutely! Or we can
just do lunch. Just asking, you look awful hungry.
Gotta go!

In the meantime, Buford is still lurking, as he tries (and tries)
to chomp down on his prey. With no luck, he winds up smacking
his gums, while shaking like a tail-feather, as fish swim (carefree)
right up to his <u>long</u> mouth-watering snout. Peek-A-Boo!
Keep playing with me! I'll gum you to death!!

Chauncey, "I don't want to be a Catfish"

Doctor, I'm so confused!
I feel trapped! like a fish out of water.
I've always felt (inside) - I should have been spawned,
as a Rainbow Trout.
I've heard of transgender re-assignment.
Is there such a thing, as fish species re-assignment?
I want to swim upstream, as a King Salmon.
For this delicate operation, I will have to cut an incision -
to perform this "fish-altering" transformation.
I don't care! – I just want to be happy!!
A "nip and tuck" here and there – and it will be <u>all</u> done.
You make it sound so simple!
I can't wait to see! what I will be, after this life-changing event!
I am going to <u>hook you up!!</u> (no pun intended).
The next time we see you – you won't be a whole catfish (anymore).
Thank-you, Doctor! Go ahead and put him to sleep.
Nurse, you handed me a scalpel, I need a fillet knife.
We're having fried catfish for dinner!
(with hush puppies on the side).
Bon Appetit!

Clyde, the "hip-hop" Cobra

All the other snake charmers, play traditional Indian street music, but Clyde only responds to "hip-hop!" Listen to him rap, "I got swag – you know I bite!" "Check out my eyes, before I strike!" And he expects me to be-bop to that!! (I wish I would!!) If he wasn't so deadly, (I swear!) I would take this flute - and shove it down his...........!! Okay! let me play something soothing, so I can relax.

While the other cobras are dancing to the movement of the flute, Clyde refuses to sway back & forth, as the (hypnotic) music plays. Instead he sulks, "I'm not budging, until you play some hip-hop!" So I have to put down my flute, and go grab a boom-box. "Can you play me some Luda?!!" Now, he's bouncing and jumping (to the beat) – as he tries to do the *"Griddy" dance* (from inside the basket). "Let's get this basket moving!"

I give up!!

Duke, you Low-down dirty dog

You itch and you scratch,
until the fleas take a nap.
You mangy mutt -
sitting on <u>my</u> front porch.
You're not full-bred,
you're full of bread.
Stop! your yapping bark and no bite,
it's interrupting <u>my</u> sleep at night.
Someone called from my phone,
to find a dog a new home.
The dog-catcher replied,
"I don't allow mangy mutts
in my ride." *Why?* 'cause you're
a low-down dirty dog.

Dunston, the "smart ass" Donkey

Dunston, this is your <u>third</u> time in the 4th grade -
....................And the school year is almost over.
You know what! I got this!! You almost passed
the last time. I hope you pass (this time around).
They say, the third time is the charm. We'll see –
Are you ready for your final exam? Bring it on!
For you – we are grading on a curve. All you
have to do is get <u>one</u> right. (Bet!)
First question: 2+0 = ?
Answer: 20
Next question: Complete the alphabet? A,B,C,D ?
Answer: E-I-E-I-O
Next question: 7x11 = ?
Answer: 7-Eleven, that's where I go to get my Slurpee on!
Let's continue,.............are you prepared to answer the next
and <u>final</u> question? Don't I look ready!
Final question: If the clock is a half-past 12:00 noon, what time is it?
Answer: Lunchtime
Did I pass? Let's just say – do you like the desk you're currently
sitting in right now? Yes! I do. Guess what? You'll be in the same seat
next year. Have a great summer!

Ellie, the forgetful Elephant

What's my name?
I don't remember -
I <u>fricking</u> don't remember!
Ella Fitzpatrick?
No, that's not it, that's not my name.
I'm thinking, it starts with an <u>E</u>.
Could it be Ethel?
No, it's not Ethel.
You know, elephants do not forget.
Really? Who told you that?
Maybe, you should get a name tag.
Okay, what name should I put?
I don't know! – how 'bout Elephant?
You are <u>no</u> help!

Elroy, the Elephant "in the Room"

Let's play! - Hide & Go, Seek!!
You-all go hide! – while I count to 10.
1, 2, 3, 4, 5,.....................
Ready, or not – Here I come!
Elroy, I see you!! "How did you find me?!!"
Well, you <u>hid</u> behind a see-through (shower) curtain!
"I think you cheated!"   <u>Seriously</u>?!!   Oh!...so now, you <u>MAD</u>!!
Guess what?!! You're the <u>only</u> elephant in the room.

Esther, the MAD Cow

Who in their right mind, would feed a herd of cattle! Steak & Eggs?!!
Look Ma! It's cousin Wilbur. No baby! Cousin Wilbur is a steer.
He's over there in the (other) pen, with the rest of the bulls –
that are a little queer.
(You know) I have just about had it with the farmer and his wife.
Every time, (when) they run out of bales of hay, they start
feeding us "Steak & Eggs."
They try to justify it by saying, it's <u>grass</u>-<u>fed</u> <u>beef</u>.
I guess you can say, it's "All-You-Can-Eat!"
I'm so MAD!!.......and upset! I'll be over here -
grazing in the grass, until I calm down.
That's bull_____!! (really it is!)

Felicia, the talking Parrot

Come on in! You're here to check-out the laptop computer.
It sounds like such a great deal! Is the bird included?
No, that's just my talking parrot, Felicia. Say Hi! Felicia.
Hi! Felicia.
Please be extremely careful what you say, this stupid parrot
repeats everything. Stupid! Huh?
I'm going to let you hear how <u>stupid I am!</u>
Computer doesn't work
Computer doesn't work
Computer doesn't work
Sucker
Sucker
Sucker
Computer doesn't work
Computer doesn't work
Computer doesn't work
Sucker
Sucker
Sucker
I'm sorry, but I don't think (that) I'm still interested in
buying this laptop. Don't listen to this dumb parrot!
It sounds to good to be true – only $23.00?
Wait, I'll even throw in this talking bird.
Sorry, but I've gotta go.
Thanks! Felicia -
Don't thank me, I'm just a dumb parrot -
All I know how to say is -
Hi! Felicia.
Bye! Felicia.

Fernando, the Gay Lion

Mama, go out and get me something to eat. I'll be right here - grooming my paws, and primping my hair. Don't hate! - you're just jealous, because I have hair and you don't!! You WISH!! you can get your nails done and your hair did!!..............So you can stop rolling your eyes – the King of the Jungle has spoken.

Because I am!........*Fernando, "The <u>Fabulous</u> Feline!!"*

Hear me <u>*ROAR!!!*</u>

Yes! your Majesty, should I bow? or would it be more appropriate - two snaps and a circle? (And) Oh! by the way – those pretty nails you have – are Claws!! for hunting prey. Funny?!! I thought you did that! Now go on with you and your home girls, and bring me back one of those fine male zebras with the broad stripes. You know, I just love a zebra in stripes.

Frieda, the Oven-roasted Turkey

Frieda, it's kind of early to be getting dressed (and ready).
I have to go to this all-day affair – it's a benefit to support the family.
Really?
Who invited you? I received quite a few invitations, (specifically)
it's for a great cause to give thanks!
Really?
And did you have to RSVP? No, not really, but I don't know why
everyone is constantly reminding me, that the party or event will not
start, until I arrive. I feel like the guest of honor!
Really?
Have you ever been inside a tanning booth?
No, why do you ask?
Well, I got this (funny) feeling – you are about to receive
your very first <u>golden</u> <u>brown</u> tan...............but you won't feel a thing!
Really?
OR Maybe I'm just over-reacting, because it's the fourth Thursday
in the month of November.

Geoffrey, the long-neck Giraffe

I'm here to see the Ear, Nose & Throat Specialist.
Do you have an appointment? No!
What seems to be the problem?
I can't seem to stop rolling my neck!!
I'm not sure, if we can provide the proper treatment –
(for your medical condition) – the doctor is an
ear, nose and throat specialist.
I heard you!! And...So!!
We are not licensed to treat your medical issues (with your neck).
Excuse-e-e-e-e!! Me-e-e!!
What do you mean?!! My medical issues!
I TOLD YOU that I can't stop rolling my neck……
and you think I have medical issues!!!
You know what!............You really do need to see a doctor -
here's a referral to an Ear, Nose & Throat Psychiatrist.
Ain't a damn thing wrong with your neck!

Henrietta, the dancing Hippo

I want you to –
Shake it to the left – shake to the right.
Then kick! twirl and pirouette, while
leaping over this muddy puddle,
pointing your toes gracefully.
Come to a complete stop and <u>slowly</u> roll to your feet.
Okay, I got it...................and you
want me to shimmy too?
You know what – I'm two-ton,
and you expect me to leap and pirouette?
Let me take my fat ass back <u>under</u> this water.

Jeremiah, was a Bullfrog

You know what! My name is <u>not</u> even Jeremiah!
I don't know who started calling me – Jeremiah!
My real name is: Lee Winifred Jenkins.
I'm from the South-side (of the pond).
I'm not a bullfrog, either - I'm a Prince!
Just waiting for a princess (to come along), to give me a kiss!
Hey! Girl!!
You wouldn't happen to be a princess, would you?
My first name is: Princess. I'm Princess Jamika Johnson.
Come on, then!! (Pucker-up!)
(Smooch!)
Ugh! that (kiss) was wet and sloppy!
Hey! You're not a prince!
And, you're <u>no</u> princess, either.

Linda, the "You need to Listen" leaping Lizard

Listen class – line up! Please. We're going outside.
Today, we are playing leapfrog.
Doesn't that sound fun!

My good friend Leonard, the frog – developed this game.
Boy! could he jump!
Yes, Johnny! <u>But Linda</u>, I want to play on the monkey bars.
Okay! Johnny, we played on the monkey bars yesterday.
On the playground, (today) we are playing leapfrog!
You got that, Johnny!!

<u>Listen Linda</u>, I don't want to play leapfrog.
Johnny, we are not playing on the monkey bars.
<u>But Linda</u>, why can't we play on the monkey bars?
Because I said so!

<u>You're not listening</u>, <u>Linda</u>…………
<u>Listen LINDA!!</u> I want to play on the monkey bars!
Johnny, you got one more time to <u>but Linda</u> me.
Okay! Class, are we ready to go? Yes, ma'am!
Johnny, where are you going? <u>Listen, Linda</u>…………

Mae, the Funky Chicken

I have a date tonight, with Tim the Rooster.
Ugh! We need to work on your (cough!) hygiene.
Do you know why they call you the funky chicken?
Because I can <u>do</u> the funky chicken.(Look!)
No! that's not why. The <u>funk</u> is already in the air -
before you start dancing.
It's not like I sit around all-day laying eggs?!!
No, but I wish you would smell under your feathers,
before you start flapping your wings.
Okay! So.....what do I have to do to <u>groove with the funk</u>! (chant)
I want to get more funk! (singing) Groove with the funk!
I want to get more funk!
Are you done?
Maybe,........I just want to <u>move</u> with the funk! (dancing away)
I wanna get more funk! (singing)!
You're hopeless!!

Millie, the "Singing" Jailbird

Headlining! is "Our (Very Own) caged Songbird"
Here she is! Millie the "Singing" Nightingale!
Sing! Millie! Sing! (Go on girl!)

"I'm just warming up!!"...................*"despite my hostage situation!"*
"I will be featured <u>nightly</u> inside this wire bird cage. Does the audience have any requests? Please hold your applause 'til the end."

The <u>next</u> selection I will be performing is: "I want to fly away." Followed by:
"I want to be free!"
My <u>all-time</u> favorite tune (and the <u>most</u> requested encore performance) is:
"Unlock the cage door & throw away the key!" And.......
the <u>final</u> (musical) selection is: "Open this <u>damn</u> bird cage, and let me out!!"

You ASK! *"<u>Why does the caged bird sing?</u>"* I <u>sing</u>! to keep from pecking (and attacking) the ol' Bird Lady. Don't look like this jailbird, will be flying anywhere…..............anytime soon.

<u>Footnote:</u> Prose written to reflect a cynical outlook,
with a satirical perspective.

Ollie, the near-sighted Owl

Ollie, what's wrong? I can't find my contacts!

So......................where are you going?

I'm going to the grocery store, to get me something to eat.

It's nighttime, better yet – it's showtime!

WE ARE OWLS!

We go out and (we) hunt for our food.

I AM HUNGRY!

And I can't see a damn thing at night,

(without my contacts) – so I'll be back,

with some chips & dip (and a moonpie).

You'll go ahead without me.

Alright! but -

Can I get a hoot! hoot!

Oscar, the gansta' rappin' Octopus

Yo! Yo! Yo! Check it out -
I'm Oscar, the gansta' rappin' Octopus.
(Listen up!)
Down below, I can give you the 411.
Under the sea, is where you'll find me.
(Please) Take my advice................you only live twice.
Bottoms up!
Keep your nose clean –
Stay in school!!
You know how I feel – just keeping it real.
Aw Snap! hook, line & sinker –
Word!

Peaches, the thoroughbred Filly

.............And they're off!!
Peaches, why are you not running?
Running? Please! I don't run, I trot.
Do you realize we're in the Kentucky Derby?
.............And do you know, I just got brand new shoes,
and I don't have a <u>hat</u>! to accessorize my saddle cloth & bridle set.
What a fashion faux pas!
No one cares! We are here to win the race!
Listen Disc Jockey – or whatever your name is!!
I don't run, unless I'm (window) shopping at the mall.
Okay! If you pick up the pace – I promise to take you shopping.
For real! Yes, whatever you want @ JCPenney.
Oh No! Unless we're going to Macy's -
I'm not taking another step.
You're killing me!
Just wave to the crowd. You'll be fine.

Pookie, the post office-working Orangutan

I know this is your first day on the job, so we'll begin in box section.
I want you to stuff the corresponding mail in the box section area,
as quickly as you (possibly) can.
Well, you have the right idea, but it would be a lot easier, if the mail
was placed in the numbered slots with the
matching P.O. Box numbers.
Also, you managed to shove an <u>entire</u> tray of mail into one slot.
We like your attitude <u>here</u> at the Post Office. Git – R – Done!
Next, we need to train you at the Window, as a Window Clerk.
Go ahead, and help the next customer.
You have the right concept, but instead of you licking the stamp
and slapping it on your butt, it would be nice if you placed the stamp
on the envelope to expedite the mailing process.
This is just your first day, and you're a lot further
along than some of the other new hires.
Now, let's scan a few parcels. Once, we scan a parcel (or package),
normally, we don't open it and (then) step on it.
I can see that you are trying, but the customers are somewhat naive,
and expect to receive their packages undamaged.
Putting the scanner in your mouth is cute!
But we (really) need to finish
scanning these packages. I'm sensing that you
don't really care, but that's OK!
You're going to fit in quite nicely, much better
than the (last) post office worker,
we hired before you.
What a Baboon!

Rufus, the EASTER Bunny

It's that time of the year again!!
  I got to hop-along like a bunny rabbit.
    You know! I'm too <u>old</u> for this crap!
     Every year, it's the same old thing!
      Hiding frickin' Easter eggs,
     sitting in a basket filled
  with <u>fake</u> green grass,
acting like I love being around these rotten kids.
   I almost lost it! when that one kid <u>shoved</u>
<u>a carrot</u> in my face. Here! bunny! bunny!
   Oh! I gotcha (Easter) bunny!
    The day is just about over!
    I can't wait to get home -
and light-up a cigar, drink a glass of wine,
  unwind, relax and put my feet up.
   I might even nibble on some
    rabbit food.

Rusty, the "trash-talking" Raccoon

Me and my lady are going out to dinner tonight.
There's a fine-dining trash can, three blocks down the street –in a cul-de-sac.
The maître d' is always on duty, but seating is limited.
"Rusty, I'm so glad you and the Mrs. could join us for dinner (tonight)."
Should I have called ahead to make reservations for a party of two?
Reservations are not required. You know the menu changes nightly.
Are there any specials? There are <u>always</u> nightly specials!
You know <u>our</u> motto – "Hit it! and quit it!!
                    For Tonight's Menu:
We have left-over meatloaf, with <u>cold</u> au gratin potatoes.
Day-old crusty bread, with a smattering of butter.
                    Also, on the menu,
We have chewed-up carrots, tossed with raisins, along with a
Cornucopia of "mushy" mixed vegetables (on the side).
                    And for dessert,
We have (broken) chocolate cake pieces.
Mmm – Yum! Go ahead and fix me and my lady a plateful of tonight's menu
items on a trash can lid –
we'll be dining-in tonight.
Hey! You!! filthy and disgusting animals, get out of my trash can!!!
On second thought - Can we have this to go?!!

Sam (I am), the Black Sheep

Hello! Ma'am! My name is Sam. Sam I am.
How interesting? I've never met a black sheep before.
I'm one-of-a-kind, that's why they call me
the black sheep of the family. I see!
Why don't we spin our wool around, and knit
a black & white sweater together – if you know
what I mean! Oh! You're ba-a-a-a-ad! with your
sheepish grin. Or let's go weave and cut a rug.
You know what they say – once you go black -
You never go back!
Are you trying to pull the wool over my eyes?
All I want to do, is shear my wool with you.
Because I AM! Madam.
The one and only, Sam I am.

Scotty, the (boiling red-hot!!) blue lobster

Is this the local seafood restaurant – Jimmy's-By-The-Sea?
Sir, I have this coupon for a free appetizer. Yes, Sir! We will
be more than happy, to give you <u>your</u> free appetizer. Would
you like to have a seat? Better yet, how 'bout a nice (warm)
water bath – while you wait.

At the bottom of that pot of boiling water (over there) -
go ahead and pick out your <u>free</u> appetizer. Do you like crabs?
I <u>love</u> crabs! Okay! then go on and climb inside the pot.
We'll be right back with your plate.

Sheila, the "Swamp" Rat

I am Sheila!!
the Queen of the "Swamp."
"All Hail the Queen!!"
Summon all my royal subjects -
"We're moving!"
Yes! Your Majesty -
the "Swamp Queen" has spoken!

Oh! *Sheila?!!*
Why are we moving?
We're moving into a larger time-share,
in the Florida Everglades.
Are you not happy here?

Have you ever heard of the
Louisiana Purchase?
Nope!
Good! I just sold our habitat,
in the Louisiana swamp,
(*On Twitter*)
as Ocean-front Swamp(land).
Grab (all) your belongings -
We've got to get the hell-up!
Outta here!!

Skeeter, the Skunk

"Now it's time to ASK Skeeter!"
Hi! I'm Skeeter, the Skunk – I would like for you
to try my <u>new</u> *de Funk Skunk cologne.*
(Lets open up the phone lines.)
Skeeter, <u>How do I get out of school detention</u>?
Spray my (new) *de Funk Skunk cologne.*
Skeeter, <u>How do I get out of jury duty</u>?
Spray my (new) *de Funk Skunk cologne.*
Skeeter, <u>How do I get out of a traffic ticket</u>?
Spray my (new) *de Funk Skunk cologne.*
keeter, <u>How do I get my Mother-in-law to move out</u>?
Spray my (new) *de Funk Skunk cologne.*
Skeeter, <u>How do I get my kids to stay outside & play</u> ('til dark)?
Spray my (new) *de Funk Skunk cologne.*
<u>*Before we go to a commercial break*</u> -
Please grab one of those scratch & sniff samples
And get a <u>good</u> whiff! of the <u>alluring</u> new fragrance and female scent -
"She de Funk (Stinkin' Skunk)" perfume.
Buy some today!

Sylvester, the Sly Fox

I'm looking for someone to watch-over my chicken coop.
It seems, my hens are escaping thru <u>that</u> gaping hole in the chicken wire.
If you accept the job – I need <u>you</u> to patch it up!
Most definitely!!

Are you interested?
Do I get a lunch break? Of, Course!
But you can't take your lunch (or dinner), inside the chicken coop.
You know the ol' adage, (laughing!)
<u>"A fox in the henhouse</u>."
No worries! I'm on a keto diet.
That's good to know -

Are there any other questions?
I was (just) thinking.......before we "patch-up" that gaping hole -
Why don't I just <u>patrol</u> (the area) right outside the chicken wire <u>fence</u> -
and "help" those hens back inside the (chicken) coop.
That might work! (I hadn't even thought about that!)
You know, you're as sly as a fox!
I know!!

Thurston, the "Can I get my Grub-On" billy goat.

Today, we are conducting a marketing research study. This will be a blind-taste test. Before, we get started–Please place your blind-folds over your eyes. That's for everyone participating, including you, Mr. Billy Goat. In front of you is Sample A. Please taste and give us your honest opinion and feedback. Next, is Sample B, and the last blind-taste test is Sample C.

Mr. Billy Goat, how did you like Sample A? Did you enjoy it? Yep! How 'bout Sample B? Yep! and Sample C ? Yep! Excuse me for asking, but did you <u>not</u> taste the difference(s) between samples A, B & C. Nope! (Not really). Well, Sample A – was a medium rare filet mignon, with a peppercorn-crusted (cream) sauce - over truffle and garlic mashed potatoes. Sample B – was an old pair of dirty socks, and Sample C – was a rotten banana peel - inside an empty shoe-box. The shoe-box <u>was</u> quite tasty!

You pretty much destroyed my marketing research study. Pretty much! Do you have anything else you would like to add? What are you going to do with this blind-fold? I could use a snack!

Vern, the Vegetarian Shark

I don't eat meat, and I <u>don't</u> like seafood,
and I think I might be allergic to shellfish.
Occasionally, I will try Sushi, only if it's
prepared with floating organic seaweed,
home-grown and harvested locally, of course.

The other day, I was out for a morning swim,
and I noticed these sharks circling above me,
in such a frenzy! So I watched to see what
was going on?...............only to find out – they
were munching and snacking on day-old chum!
How disgusting!! I almost gagged! when one of
them offered me left-over fish-bones.

Vincent, the <u>fly</u>-on-the-wall

I see everything!
I <u>know</u> everything!
Did Cassondra get a promotion?
Yes, she did! It's not what you know -
but who you know!...........
And she knows the boss quite well!
Did Cecil get fired? Yep!
........and he left crying like a baby!
They keep trying to <u>shoo</u> me
out of the conference room, but
I just hide in the closet.
You know who else is (hiding)
in the closet? I'm not saying,
but he works a lot of overtime -
if you know what I mean!
Is the new girl taking over Cassondra's position?
Yes, but not all of them;
just the job-related position.
                    Hello!

Walter, the bald Eagle

I would like to inquire about a hair transplant?
Name? Walter.
Occupation? I fly for a living.
Next of Kin? My brother attends Auburn University,
                and goes by the nickname, "War Eagle."
Eyesight? Yes
Vision? I can see clearly now, the rains are gone.
Any Phobias? I used to be afraid of heights, but now
             I'm terrified of that big metal bird.
So you're terrified of an airplane.
What's an airplane?
Never mind, next question.
Family Medical History? Baldness.
Do you suffer from Male-pattern baldness?
I'm bald – but it doesn't come in a pattern.
Does you bald-spot cause you any discomfort,
or make you sore?
Yes, I was soaring just the other day, and I flew
from the mountain ledge to the treetop,
for no apparent reason.
Okay! Does Alopecia run in your family?
No one runs in our family –
We all fly!

Footnote: Walter, you stupid!

Willie, the fat-belly Hog

Look at me!
You ain't never seen such a <u>BIG</u> Sexy
and succulent round mound of pounds!
I'm fat, sweaty and plump!
....and I love to roll around "skinny dipping" in a waterbed of slop.
Look at me!
From head to tail -
I'm like a fine wine of swine.
I'm so fine, that I can't stand myself!
(Strike a pose)
Now feast your eyes on this!
The ladies call me – Hog Wild,
but you can just call me Willie.

<u>Salute</u>

I wish to express
my appreciation and
sincere gratitude
<u>to the entire staff</u>
of
<u>Author Reputation Press, LLC</u>;
with Special recognition
to:
Ms. Elle Murray, Fulfillment Officer.

"They will make war against the Lamb,
but the Lamb will overcome them because
he is Lord of lords and King of kings -
and with him will be his called,
chosen and faithful followers."

Revelation 17:14

-*Poetic Ending*-

Reflections

Elmo, the flying Monkey

Looking back!........I wonder -
if I qualify!! for unemployment?

I used to have a steady gig -
working for a wicked ol' witch!

But the gig dried up – when she
melted into a puddle of water.

I tried to find work –
walking this lil girl's dog.
But she said, "No thanks!"
"I'm good."

Why would anyone name their dog – Toto?
That does "Shock" the monkey!

With all this new construction (going on!)
The yellow-brick road is now a toll-road.
I guess, I'll fly-over!

Well, let me see if I (can) find myself,
(some) steady employment.
In the meantime...........
Peace Out!!

I can do all things through him
who strengths me.
Philippians 4:13

Dedication

You feel me

I'm up here on this operating table -
They gon' cut me sho' nuff.
I'ma play dead, see if they leave.
Oh! no! here he come!
Ya'll need to go 'head
…and put me to sleep.
Ma'am, are you okay?
Look! I need more time.
What I got? <u>I can live with it!</u>
Go cut somebody else.
You feel me!
Cancel the bunion surgery
in Room 2B.

This book is dedicated

to my cousin, Mrs. Geraldine Bowers;

in loving memory of her eldest son, "Mickey"

Through Christ
with an undeniable
Trust in GOD
we were able to achieve
such literary succcess.

Special thanks! to Veronica & Anthony, and his dog, Ace.

Afterthought and Spiritual Guidance

What the Hail!!!

I walk outside and see
these small ice balls.
Pounding the sidewalk
and dinging all these cars.
It can't be snow!!
...............for all I know -
What the hell is it?
I mean,
what the hail is this!!
Confused raindrops
shaped like golf balls.
I listen to the tinging
atop my rooftop and
I ask myself, if God is
crying - he <u>must</u> have
cracked his side......But it
couldn't have been <u>that</u> funny.

Be of good courage, and
he shall strengthen your heart,
all ye that hope in the LORD.

Psalm 31:24

Final Thought

Live or Let Die!

A life that doesn't live,
sits and watches me cry.
A life that doesn't live,
should either live – or let die!
A life that doesn't live,
stands in the shadows of love.
A life that doesn't live,
flutters away..........like a dove.
A life that doesn't live,
wakes up each morning to pray!
A life that doesn't live
Hopefully, it will change today!!

For The
Word Of The
Cross
IS THE POWER OF GOD!

.........He said to Peter -

"Put out into deep water, and let down the nets for a catch."

Peter answered:

"Master, we've worked hard all night and haven't caught anything."
"But because you say so, I will let down the nets."

Excerpt from Luke 5: 4-5

Book Summary
Poems 31 -

A collection of poems & prose, which showcase my talents
as a writer and poet. Each poem (or prose) brings to life a
writing and poetic style, which embraces my own unique way
of sharing my creative thoughts and feelings through writing.
I write to tantalize the reader's interest through poetry (or prose).

Each poem (or prose) may have a different rhythm or rhyme,
but each poetic composition possesses workmanship quality.
My thoughts are - that I can challenge and stimulate the
readers to think creatively about the true
meaning of each poem (or prose).

Though, I started out writing poetry, then prose – a new form
of creative writing developed/evolved into what I call <u>S</u>TUPID!
<u>S</u>TAND-<u>U</u>P (Comedy) <u>IN</u> <u>D</u>ICTION. This (new) bold style of
writing is very prevalent in the latter Chapters added
(4 & 5), especially Chapter 5 - "Animal Crackers."

Otherwise, I just want you to simply enjoy the pleasure
of reading and enjoying my literary work.

Author Biography

Meet the Author

Donald Anthony King—This writer retired as a Commander (in April 2004) from the Naval Reserves, after 22 years of military service. He graduated from Florida State University (FSU) in December 1981, with a Bachelor's (B.S.) degree, after transferring from Florida A&M University (FAMU), with an Associate of Arts (A.A.) degree. His Master's (M.S.) degree was attained (July 2010) from the satellite Tyndall AFB branch of TROY University, in Panama City, Florida. He and his family currently live in Austin, Texas.

Acknowledgments

Poet/Author/Editor
Donald Anthony King

"Thank You"

READERS

Charlotte, the "Voluptuous" Miss P.I.G.

Make-up!! Please!
20 minutes 'til Showtime!!
Miss P.I.G.?!! Do you wear this color red?
I've never put lipstick on a pig (before) -
You look! Mar-ve-lous!!

Sir Cole B., the Arctic Penguin

I'm not illin', just Stone-cold chillin'
I might have just spotted my soul-mate?!!
Hey! Mama! You want to slide
down the slope with me?
Only, if you jump off a "jagged" iceberg – Head first!
(into the ocean).
Try not to hit your head!!
That's cold!!!

I express my deepest gratitude
and "Thanks!" to all of you-
who allowed me to share my creative journey
with you!

The End